SCOTT FORESMAN READING STREET
Writing and Research Handbook
GRADE 4

COMMON CORE EDITION ©

P9-DEH-384

Copyright © Pearson Education, Inc., or its affiliates. All Rights Reserved. Printed in the United States of America. This publication is protected by copyright, and permission should be obtained from the publisher prior to any prohibited reproduction, storage in a retrieval system, or transmission in any form or by any means, electronic, mechanical, photocopying, recording, or likewise. The publisher hereby grants permission to reproduce these pages, in part or in whole, for classroom use only, the number not to exceed the number of students in each class. Notice of copyright must appear on all copies. For information regarding permissions, write to Pearson Curriculum Group Rights & Permissions, One Lake Street, Upper Saddle River, New Jersey 07458.

Pearson, Scott Foresman, and Pearson Scott Foresman are trademarks, in the U.S. and/or other countries, of Pearson Education, Inc., or its affiliates.

Common Core State Standards: © Copyright 2010. National Governors Association Center for Best Practices and Council of Chief State School Officers. All rights reserved.

ISBN-13: 978-0-328-68632-2
ISBN-10:   0-328-68632-8
5 6 7 8 9 10 V0N4 19 18 17 16 15 14 13

Glenview, Illinois

Boston, Massachusetts

Chandler, Arizona

Upper Saddle River, New Jersey

Table of Contents

Unit 1 Turning Points

Narrative Writing

Introduce and Brainstorm 4

Narrow the Topic 5

Gather Information 6

Organize Information 7

Revise, Edit, and Evaluate 8

Publish and Extend 9

Unit 2 Teamwork

Writing an Opinion

Introduce and Brainstorm 10

Narrow the Topic 11

Gather Information 12

Organize Information 13

Revise, Edit, and Evaluate 14

Publish and Extend 15

Unit 3 Patterns in Nature

Expository Writing

Introduce and Brainstorm 16

Narrow the Topic 17

Gather Information 18

Organize Information 19

Revise, Edit, and Evaluate 20

Publish and Extend 21

Unit 4 Puzzles and Mysteries

Narrative Writing

Introduce and Brainstorm 22

Narrow the Topic 23

Gather Information 24

Organize Information 25

Revise, Edit, and Evaluate 26

Publish and Extend 27

Unit 5 Adventures in Nature

Expository Writing

Introduce and Brainstorm 28

Narrow the Topic 29

Gather Information 30

Organize Information 31

Revise, Edit, and Evaluate 32

Publish and Extend 33

Unit 6 Reaching for Goals

Writing an Opinion

Introduce and Brainstorm 34

Narrow the Topic 35

Gather Information 36

Organize Information 37

Revise, Edit, and Evaluate 38

Publish and Extend 39

Blackline Masters

Graphic Organizer Web

Think About Audience, Purpose, and Organization 41

Gather Information 42

Basic Outline 43

Opinion Outline 44

Evaluation Form/Narrative 45

Evaluation Form/Expository 46

Evaluation Form/Opinion 47

UNIT 1: TURNING POINTS

Introduce the Writing Assignment

Tell students that they will be writing a narrative. Explain that a **narrative** is a story about characters. The story tells what the characters do. For example, the story of Thomas Jefferson and John Adams writing the Declaration of Independence is a narrative. The narrative tells what happens to these characters. The characters have a problem or goal. The events that happen as they solve the problem or achieve their goal make up the plot. The place or places where the events occur is the setting.

The Writing of the Declaration of Independence	
Characters	Thomas Jefferson and John Adams
Setting	Independence Hall in Philadelphia, 1776
Plot	John Adams and Thomas Jefferson are appointed to a committee to draft the Declaration of Independence. John Adams insists that Jefferson, a man of letters, ought to write it personally.

Point out that a narrative about how the Declaration of Independence was written is nonfiction because it tells about real characters and events. A fiction narrative tells about imaginary characters and events. Every narrative has characters, a plot, and a setting.

Brainstorm Topics

Remind students that the first step in writing is to think of a **topic** to write about. One way to generate topic ideas is to brainstorm, or work together to come up with as many ideas as possible. Distribute copies of the web on page 40 to students. Remind them that the theme of Unit 1 is Turning Points, and write *Turning Points* in the center oval. Ask students to think of events that might be turning points, or occasions when important changes occur. Write students' answers in the ovals of the web. Prompt with questions such as *What turning points might people your age experience? How can historical events be turning points? How might doing something successfully be a turning point?*

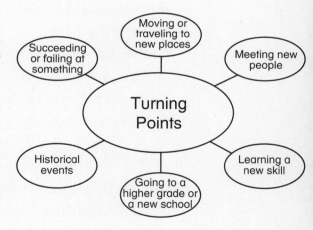

CCSS Writing 3. Write narratives to develop real or imagined experiences or events using effective technique, descriptive details, and clear event sequences.
CCSS Speaking/Listening 1. Engage effectively in a range of collaborative discussions (one-on-one, in groups, and teacher-led) with diverse partners *on grade 4 topics and texts*, building on others' ideas and expressing their own clearly.

Narrow the Topic

Display the web of topics that the class constructed. Ask students to suggest specific story ideas, both fiction and nonfiction, for each of the general topics. For example, "A boy learns to swim" or "The Founding Fathers write the Declaration of Independence."

After brainstorming topics, students need to choose one of the topics to write about. They also need to consider the following:

- Is the topic the right size for your narrative? There should be just enough characters and events so that the story is not too short or too long.
- Do you already have ideas about the characters and events? Before you begin brainstorming or researching details, you should have characters, a setting, and events in mind.

If the answer to either question is no, encourage students to choose another topic.

Once students have chosen their topics, it is time for them to start planning their writing. First, they need to think about their audience and purpose for writing. Distribute copies of page 41 to students. Ask students to answer the two questions at the top of the page. Explain that they should keep their audience and purpose in mind while they are planning and writing their first drafts.

Next, students need to begin writing and organizing the plot of their narratives. Ask them to write any events they have already thought of and then sort those into *More Important* and *Less Important*. This will help them both to evaluate the events of their plots and to see how much brainstorming or research they need to do to find more.

CCSS Writing 3.a. Orient the reader by establishing a situation and introducing a narrator and/or characters; organize an event sequence that unfolds naturally.
CCSS Writing 4. Produce clear and coherent writing in which the development and organization are appropriate to task, purpose, and audience.

Gather Information

Distribute copies of the chart on page 42 to students. Remind them that **research** provides useful information from sources such as print material and Web sites. In the columns on the chart, model how to write the source information and then make notes about the characters (John Adams, Thomas Jefferson, a Congressional committee), the setting (Congress, 1775), the problem (writing the Declaration of Independence), and the events (A committee chooses Jefferson and Adams to write the Declaration of Independence. Adams tells Jefferson that Jefferson should write it. Jefferson does. Adams is happy with it and doesn't revise it.).

If students are writing fictional stories, tell them to imagine the settings and the events in their plots and brainstorm details for both. Suggest using dialogue to make the narratives vivid. Point out that students may need to find facts for nonfiction narratives or to support details in fictional stories. Guide them to current print material and reliable Web sites. Ask students to write facts and details on the chart under "Information." Explain that if they brainstorm the details, they can write "myself" under "Source." If they get facts from another source, they record it under "Source."

Allow time for students to brainstorm and/or research details and facts to use in their narratives.

CCSS Writing 3.b. Use dialogue and description to develop experiences and events or show the responses of characters to situations. CCSS Writing 8. Recall relevant information from experiences or gather relevant information from print and digital sources; take notes and categorize information, and provide a list of sources.

Organize Information

Tell students that after they have gathered enough events and details for their narratives, they need to organize all this information so they can begin writing. One way they can do this is to make an **outline.**

Distribute copies of the outline on page 43 to students. Use the following information or information from a selection you've read in class to model how to begin an outline for students.

I. Introduction Someone must write the Declaration of Independence.

II. Body

> **A.** A Congressional committee chooses Adams and Jefferson.

> **B.** Adams asks Jefferson to write the Declaration.

> **C.** Jefferson writes the Declaration.

III. Conclusion Adams is happy with Jefferson's work.

Explain that students may need to add or delete numbers or letters in the outline to suit their particular information.

Have students use their outlines to write the **first drafts** of their narratives. Encourage them to write one paragraph for the introduction, one paragraph for the body, and one paragraph for the conclusion.

© **Grade 4**

CCSS Writing 3.e. Provide a conclusion that follows from the narrated experiences or events.

Revise, Edit, and Evaluate Writing

Remind students that the goal of a first draft is to get their ideas down on paper without worrying about everything being right. After they have finished writing their first drafts, they will revise and edit their writing before making final drafts.

Explain that when they **revise** their writing, students look at the words they chose, the kinds of sentences they wrote, and how they organized their ideas. They decide whether they need to rearrange sentences for clear time order. They might add questions or exclamations for greater sentence variety. They might add dialogue to make the characters and events vivid.

When they **edit** their writing, students look for errors in spelling, punctuation, capitalization, and grammar. Suggest that students look for one type of mistake at a time and that they keep a dictionary handy to check word spellings. Other editing strategies include reading aloud to themselves or to a partner and placing a ruler or card under each line to help them focus on the words in that line.

Display page 45 and distribute copies to students. Tell them to use the checklists at the top of the page to help them know what to look for as they revise and edit their first drafts. Allow time for them to revise and edit their writing.

Ask students to write **final drafts** incorporating their revisions and corrections. Then have them answer the questions at the bottom of page 45 to help them focus on what they like about their writing and what they want to improve.

Ⓒ **Grade 4**

CCSS Writing 5. With guidance and support from peers and adults, develop and strengthen writing as needed by planning, revising, and editing. **CCSS Language 1.** Demonstrate command of the conventions of standard English grammar and usage when writing or speaking. **CCSS Language 2.** Demonstrate command of the conventions of standard English capitalization, punctuation, and spelling when writing.

Publish and Extend Writing

Tell students that when they **publish** their writing, they share it with others. Explain that there are many different ways that writers can publish their writing. Offer these ideas for publishing, and encourage students to think of and implement their own ideas.

Ways to Publish

- Exchange and read narratives in a group. As a group, explain how each narrative illustrates a turning point. Pose and respond to questions about one another's narratives.

- Read a partner's narrative. Describe three features you especially liked.

- Read the narrative aloud to the class. Have your classmates identify the story's main characters, setting, problem, and solution.

- Create a class bulletin board called "Turning Points." Group the narratives by similar topics.

- As a class, choose two or three narratives to dramatize.

Tell students that when they **extend** their writing, they go beyond what they were asked to do in the writing assignment. Offer these ideas for extending, and encourage students to think of and implement their own ideas.

Ways to Extend

- If you wrote a fictional story, write a nonfiction story with the theme of turning points, and vice versa.

- Write a second narrative that describes a different turning point for the story's characters.

- Write the narrative in play form, using only stage directions and dialogue to tell the story.

- Find a story in the library with the theme of turning points. Write a summary of the story.

- Write an alternate ending for the narrative. Share both endings with a partner and discuss which ending is better.

Ⓒ **Grade 4**

CCSS Writing 6. Use technology, including the Internet, to produce and publish writing as well as to interact and collaborate with others; demonstrate sufficient command of keyboarding skills to type a minimum of three pages in a single sitting. **CCSS Speaking/Listening 1.c.** Pose and respond to specific questions with elaboration and detail by making comments that contribute to the topic, text, or issue under discussion.

UNIT 2: TEAMWORK

Introduce the Writing Assignment

Tell students that they will be writing an opinion. Explain that an **opinion** is what a person thinks about something. Offer these examples: *Jeffrey thinks that teamwork is the best way to achieve a goal. Maria thinks searching for a solution on the Internet is the best way to achieve a goal.* These are Jeffrey's and Maria's opinions about this topic. Their opinions cannot be proven to be true, like facts can. However, Jeffrey and Maria can give reasons and details that support their opinions. Share their reasons and details with students.

Jeffrey's Opinion: Teamwork is the best way to achieve a goal.	Maria's Opinion: Searching on the Internet is the best way to achieve a goal.
Supporting Reasons and Details: A winning team needs more than one good player. I once sold lemonade with my brothers to pay for a vase I broke.	**Supporting Reasons and Details:** There is a lot of useful information on the Web. I once found advice on how to unclog a drain on the Web.

Point out that Jeffrey and Maria can use their reasons and details not only to explain their opinions about the best way to achieve a goal, but also to try to convince others to agree with their opinions.

Brainstorm Topics

Remind students that the first step in writing is to think of a **topic** to write about. One way to generate topic ideas is to brainstorm, or work together to come up with as many ideas as possible. Distribute copies of the web on page 40 to students. Remind them that the theme of Unit 2 is Teamwork, and write *Teamwork* in the center oval. Ask students to think of groups that demonstrate teamwork. Write students' answers next to the outer ovals of the web. Then ask them about opinions they might have about each group. Prompt with questions such as *In what kinds of jobs must people use teamwork? What kinds of animals demonstrate teamwork?* Encourage students to answer using words and phrases that express opinions (*I think; I believe; most important; should*) and write them on the web.

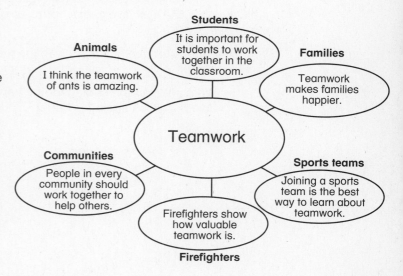

Students
It is important for students to work together in the classroom.

Animals
I think the teamwork of ants is amazing.

Families
Teamwork makes families happier.

Teamwork

Communities
People in every community should work together to help others.

Sports teams
Joining a sports team is the best way to learn about teamwork.

Firefighters
Firefighters show how valuable teamwork is.

Ⓒ Grade 4

CCSS Writing 1. Write opinion pieces on topics or texts, supporting a point of view with reasons and information. CCSS Speaking Listening 1. Engage effectively in a range of collaborative discussions (one-on-one, in groups, and teacher-led) with diverse partners *on grade 4 topics and texts*, building on others' ideas and expressing their own clearly.

Narrow the Topic

Display the web of topics that the class constructed. Review the opinions and why they are opinions. Point out the use of words such as *important, happier, best, valuable, should,* and *think,* and explain that students can use words such as these to identify opinions.

After brainstorming topics, students need to choose one of the topics to write about. They also need to consider the following:

- Is the topic the right size for your opinion writing? The topic should be neither too big nor too small.

- Do you already know something about the topic? Even before you begin researching, you should be able to think of some supporting reasons and details.

If the answer to either question is no, encourage students to choose another topic.

Once students have chosen their topics, it is time for them to start planning their writing. First, they need to think about their audience and purpose for writing. Distribute copies of page 41 to students. Ask students to answer the two questions at the top of the page. Explain that they should keep their audience and purpose in mind while they are planning and writing their first drafts.

Next, students need to begin writing and organizing their reasons and details. Ask them to write any reasons and details they have already thought of and then sort those into *More Important* and *Less Important.* This will help them both to evaluate their reasons and details and to see how much research they need to do to find more.

Ⓒ **Grade 4**

CCSS Writing 1.a. Introduce a topic or text clearly, state an opinion, and create an organizational structure in which related ideas are grouped to support the writer's purpose. **CCSS Writing 1.b.** Provide reasons that are supported by facts and details. **CCSS Writing 4.** Produce clear and coherent writing in which the development and organization are appropriate to task, purpose, and audience.

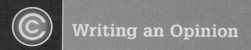
Gather Information

Distribute copies of the chart on page 42 to students. Remind them that **research** provides useful information from sources such as print material and Web sites. To help students look for facts to support the opinions they have chosen to write about, guide them to current print material and reliable Web sites. Point out that they can also use information from their own or others' experiences. Model by finding facts to support the opinion "The best way to achieve a goal is through teamwork," such as facts by an expert about teams or teamwork in a nonfiction book or an interview with one or more people. Add information about these sources (book title, author's name; date and participants of interview) to the chart. Then place the details that support the opinion (siblings who do chores together finish them more quickly; putting together a lemonade stand with friends is a good way to make some money) into the chart, explaining what you are doing and why.

Allow time for students to research reasons, details, and facts to use in their opinion writing.

Ⓒ **Grade 4**

CCSS Writing 9. Draw evidence from literary or informational texts to support analysis, reflection, and research.

Organize Information

Tell students that after they have gathered enough reasons, details, and facts to support their opinions, they need to organize this information. One way they can organize their information is to make an **outline.**

Distribute copies of the outline on page 44 to students. Use the following information or information from a selection you've read in class to model how to begin an outline for students.

Topic Teamwork: using teamwork to achieve goals

Opinion The best way to achieve a goal is through teamwork.

A. Reason 1 There are real-life examples of how teamwork achieves goals.

1. Supporting detail It takes more than just one good player to make a winning team.

2. Supporting detail Siblings that do chores together finish them quicker.

Explain that students may need to add or delete numbers or letters in the outline to suit their particular information. Have students use their outlines to write the **first drafts** of their opinions. Encourage them to write one paragraph for the introduction, one paragraph for each reason, and one paragraph for the conclusion.

CCSS Writing 8. Recall relevant information from experiences or gather relevant information from print and digital sources; take notes and categorize information, and provide a list of sources.

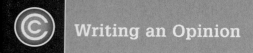

Revise, Edit, and Evaluate Writing

Remind students that the goal of a first draft is to get their ideas down on paper without worrying about everything being right. After they have finished writing their first drafts, they will revise and edit their writing before making final drafts.

Explain that when they **revise** their writing, students look at the words they chose, the kinds of sentences they wrote, and how they organized their ideas. They decide whether all of their sentences support the main idea and are organized from least important reason to most important reason. They might divide some sentences in two or combine some sentences for greater variety. They might change passive voice to active voice and use vivid action verbs.

When they **edit** their writing, students look for errors in spelling, punctuation, capitalization, and grammar. Suggest that students look for one type of mistake at a time and that they keep a dictionary handy to check word spellings. Other editing strategies include reading aloud to themselves or to a partner and placing a ruler or card under each line to help them focus on the words in that line.

Distribute copies of page 47 to students. Tell them to use the checklists at the top of the page to help them know what to look for as they revise and edit their first drafts. Allow time for them to revise and edit their writing.

Ask students to write **final drafts** incorporating their revisions and corrections. Then have them answer the questions at the bottom of page 47 to help them focus on what they like about their writing and what they want to improve.

Ⓒ Grade 4

CCSS Writing 5. With guidance and support from peers and adults, develop and strengthen writing as needed by planning, revising, and editing. CCSS Language 1. Demonstrate command of the conventions of standard English grammar and usage when writing or speaking. CCSS Language 2. Demonstrate command of the conventions of standard English capitalization, punctuation, and spelling when writing.

Publish and Extend Writing

Tell students that when they **publish** their writing, they share it with others. Explain that there are many different ways that writers can publish their writing. Offer these ideas for publishing, and encourage students to think of and implement their own ideas.

Ways to Publish

- Give an oral presentation of your opinion writing to classmates. Answer questions about the reasons for your opinion.

- Make a bulletin board titled "Opinions." Display your writing and illustrations.

- Ask family members for opinions on the issue you wrote about. Then share and discuss your written opinion.

- Publish your opinion in a school newspaper.

- Read aloud your opinion writing to a partner. Ask the partner to agree or disagree with the opinion, giving reasons. Then switch roles with your partner.

Tell students that when they **extend** their writing, they go beyond what they were asked to do in the writing assignment. Offer these ideas for extending, and encourage students to think of and implement their own ideas.

Ways to Extend

- Research and write about two reasons that support the opposite side of your opinion.

- Read a story about teamwork. State an opinion about the story. List reasons to support the opinion.

- With a partner, choose an opinion to debate. Take turns offering reasons to support two opposite sides of the issue.

- Write a fictional story that illustrates your opinion about teamwork.

- Make a poster with illustrated reasons for your opinion.

© Grade 4

CCSS Writing 6. With some guidance and support from adults, use technology, including the Internet, to produce and publish writing as well as to interact and collaborate with others; demonstrate sufficient command of keyboarding skills to type a minimum of one page in a single sitting. CCSS Speaking Listening 1.c. Pose and respond to specific questions to clarify or follow up on information, and make comments that contribute to the discussion and link to the remarks of others.

UNIT 3: PATTERNS IN NATURE

Introduce the Writing Assignment

Tell students that they will be writing an informative/explanatory text, which is also known as expository text. Point out that an **informatative/explanatory text** has a specific topic. It states a main idea about the topic. Facts and details support the main idea. For example, a writer might tell about the importance of patterns on animals in the wild.

Topic	Patterns on animals
Main Idea	Patterns on animals serve an important purpose in the wild.
Supporting Fact	Zebras have black and white stripes that help them identify one another.
Supporting Fact	Giraffes have brown and tan markings that help camouflage and protect them from predators.
Supporting Fact	Some butterflies are able to hide from predators because the patterns on their wings look like leaves.

Point out that a writer must carefully choose supporting facts that best explain the main idea. For a short informative/explanatory text, three or four facts are usually enough.

Brainstorm Topics

Remind students that the first step in writing is to think of a **topic** to write about. One way to generate topic ideas is to brainstorm, or work together to come up with as many ideas as possible. Distribute copies of the web on page 40 to students. Remind them that the theme of Unit 3 is Patterns in Nature, and write *Patterns in Nature* in the center oval. Ask students to think of elements in nature that have patterns. Write students' answers in the ovals of the web. Prompt with questions such as *What patterns can you find in the sky? Does the ocean have patterns? What kinds of patterns do animals have?*

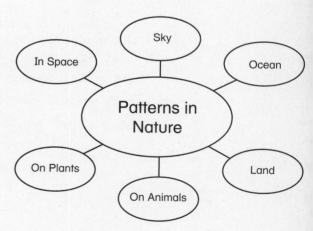

CCSS Writing 2. Write informative/explanatory texts to examine a topic and convey ideas and information clearly. **CCSS Speaking Listening 1.** Engage effectively in a range of collaborative discussions (one-on-one, in groups, and teacher-led) with diverse partners *on grade 4 topics and texts*, building on others' ideas and expressing their own clearly.

Narrow the Topic

Display the web of topics that the class constructed. Ask students to suggest specific topics for each of the general topics, such as "zebras' patterns of stripes" or "wave patterns in the ocean."

After brainstorming topics, students need to choose one of the topics to write about. Have students consider the following:

- Is the topic the right size for your informative text? The topic should be neither too big nor too small.

- Do you already know something about the topic? Even before you begin researching, you should be able to think of some supporting facts and details.

If the answer to either question is no, encourage students to choose another topic.

Once students have chosen their topics, it is time for them to start planning their writing. First, they need to think about their audience and purpose for writing. Distribute copies of page 41 to students. Ask students to answer the two questions at the top of the page. Explain that they should keep their audience and purpose in mind while they are planning and writing their first drafts.

Next, students need to begin writing and organizing their facts and details. Ask them to write any facts and details they have already thought of and then sort those into *More Important* and *Less Important*. This will help them both to evaluate their facts and details and to see how much research they need to do to find more.

CCSS Writing 4. Produce clear and coherent writing in which the development and organization are appropriate to task, purpose, and audience.

Gather Information

Distribute copies of the chart on page 42 to students. Remind them that **research** provides useful information from sources such as print material and Web sites. To help students look for facts to support their topics, guide them to current print material and reliable Web sites. Point out that they can also use information from their own or others' experiences. Model by finding facts to support the main idea "Patterns on animals serve an important purpose in the wild," such as the habits of zebras in a nonfiction book or facts about giraffes in an encyclopedia. Add information about these sources (book title, author's name; name of encyclopedia, article title, author's name) to the chart. Then record the details that support the main idea (Zebras may identify one another through each animal's unique stripes; giraffes have brown and tan markings that help camouflage them.) into the chart, explaining what you are doing and why.

Allow time for students to research details and facts to use in their informative/ explanatory writing.

Ⓒ Grade 4

CCSS Writing 9. Draw evidence from literary or informational texts to support analysis, reflection, and research.

Organize Infomation

Tell students that after they have gathered enough details and facts to support their topics, they need to organize all this information so that they can begin writing. One way they can organize their information is to make an **outline.**

Distribute copies of the outline on page 43 to students. Use the following information or information from a selection you've read in class to model how to begin an ourline for students.

I. Introduction Zebras and giraffes have unique patterns.

II. Body

    A. Zebras have black and white stripes.

        1. Zebras' stripes blend together when they are in large groups.

        2. The stripes help camouflage zebras from predators.

Explain that students may need to add or delete numbers or letters in the outline to suit their particular information.

Have students use their outlines to write the **first drafts** of their informative/explanatory text. Encourage them to write one paragraph for the introduction, one paragraph for each main idea in the body, and one paragraph for the conclusion.

 Grade 4

CCSS Writing 2.a. Introduce a topic clearly and group related information in paragraphs and sections; include formatting (e.g., headings), illustrations, and multimedia when useful to aiding comprehension. **CCSS Writing 2.b.** Develop the topic with facts, definitions, concrete details, quotations, or other information and examples related to the topic. **CCSS Writing 8.** Recall relevant information from experiences or gather relevant information from print and digital sources; take notes and categorize information, and provide a list of sources.

Revise, Edit, and Evaluate Writing

Remind students that the goal of a first draft is to get their ideas down on paper without worrying about everything being right. After they have finished writing their first drafts, they will revise and edit their writing before making final drafts.

Explain that when they **revise** their writing, students look at the words they chose, the kinds of sentences they wrote, and how they organized their ideas. They decide whether their sentences are organized in a logical order, such as time order or order of importance. They decide whether to add details to make their writing more vivid. They might delete details or sentences that do not support their topics.

When they **edit** their writing, students look for errors in spelling, punctuation, capitalization, and grammar. Suggest that students look for one type of mistake at a time and that they keep a dictionary handy to check word spellings. Other editing strategies include reading aloud to themselves or to a partner and placing a ruler or card under each line to help them focus on the words in that line.

Distribute copies of page 46 to students. Tell them to use the checklists at the top of the page to help them know what to look for as they revise and edit their first drafts. Allow time for them to revise and edit their writing.

Ask students to write **final drafts** incorporating their revisions and corrections. Then have them answer the questions at the bottom of page 46 to help them focus on what they like about their writing and what they want to improve.

© Grade 4

CCSS Writing 5. With guidance and support from peers and adults, develop and strengthen writing as needed by planning, revising, and editing. CCSS Language 1. Demonstrate command of the conventions of standard English grammar and usage when writing or speaking. CCSS Language 2. Demonstrate command of the conventions of standard English capitalization, punctuation, and spelling when writing.

Publish and Extend Writing

Tell students that when they **publish** their writing, they share it with others. Explain that there are many different ways that writers can publish their writing. Offer these ideas for publishing, and encourage students to think of and implement their own ideas.

Ways to Publish

- Meet in small groups organized by similar topics, such as patterns in space or patterns on plants. Read one another's informative/explanatory texts aloud and discuss each one.

- Read aloud your informative/explanatory text to the class and ask classmates to identify one or two features that were particularly well done, such as vivid descriptions or interesting facts.

- Make a drawing that artistically interprets the natural pattern described in your informative/explanatory text. Put texts and drawings in a class booklet.

- As a class, create a bulletin board with the theme Patterns in Nature. Post your illustrated informative/explanatory text.

- Take your informative/explanatory text home and invite family members and friends to read and comment on it. Share the comments in class.

Tell students that when they **extend** their writing, they go beyond what they were asked to do in the writing assignment. Offer these ideas for extending, and encourage students to think of and implement their own ideas.

Ways to Extend

- After reading or listening to others' informative/explanatory texts, choose a classmate's topic that interests you. Research new facts about the topic and write about it.

- Research two new facts or details about your topic. Add the new information to your informative/explanatory text.

- Create a web of related topics suggested by the topic of your informative/ explanatory text. Choose one to research and write about.

- Create a poster with facts and illustrations on the topic of your informative/ explanatory text.

- State an opinion about the topic of your informative/explanatory text. List three reasons to support the opinion.

© Grade 4

CCSS Writing 6. With some guidance and support from adults, use technology, including the Internet, to produce and publish writing as well as to interact and collaborate with others; demonstrate sufficient command of keyboarding skills to type a minimum of one page in a single sitting. **CCSS Speaking Listening 1.c.** Pose and respond to specific questions to clarify or follow up on information, and make comments that contribute to the discussion and link to the remarks of others.

UNIT 4: PUZZLES AND MYSTERIES

Introduce the Writing Assignment

Tell students that they will be writing a narrative. Explain that a **narrative** describes an event or tells a story. It has characters, a setting (the time and place), and a plot (a series of events). A narrative may tell about a real-life story or an invented one. Offer an example of each kind of narrative: *Scientists solve the mystery of how King Tut died. Maria solves the mystery of the missing sweatshirt.*

Setting	King Tut's pyramid tomb, Egypt, 2007–2010	Maria's home
Characters	Dr. Ashraf Selim, a team of scientists and doctors	Maria, her sister Moira, their cat Mitzi
Plot	A team uses DNA tests and X-rays to find out how the boy king died.	Maria uses logic to find her lost sweatshirt.

Point out that a narrative describes the characters, setting, and problem in the beginning, tells how this problem develops in the middle, and reveals how the characters solve it at the end.

Brainstorm Topics

As a class, have students list real-life and imaginary mysteries they could develop as **topics** for their narratives. Distribute copies of the web on page 40. Remind students that the theme of Unit 4 is Puzzles and Mysteries, and write *Puzzles and Mysteries* in the center oval. Ask students to think of historic and everyday puzzles they know about. Write their responses in the outer ovals of the web. Prompt students to tell what makes these events mystery stories with questions such as *What mystery had to be solved? Who solved it?* Encourage students to sum up each mystery in a sentence, and add the sentences to the appropriate ovals.

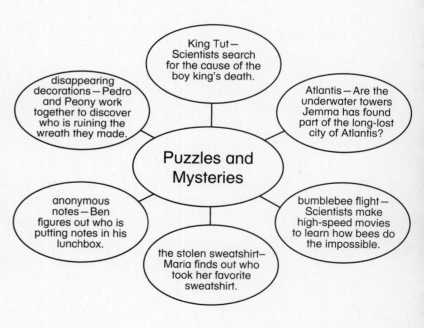

© Grade 4

CCSS Writing 3. Write narratives to develop real or imagined experiences or events using effective technique, descriptive details, and clear event sequences.
CCSS Speaking Listening 1. Engage effectively in a range of collaborative discussions (one-on-one, in groups, and teacher-led) with diverse partners *on grade 4 topics and texts*, building on others' ideas and expressing their own clearly.

Narrow the Topic

Review the web that the class constructed. Explain that students need to choose one of the mysteries to write a story about. To help students get a sense of each mystery, work together to create introductions that establish the setting, characters, and conflict for each topic. For example,

"JANE!" I shouted at my little sister. "Stop taking my clothes!!" My favorite blue sweatshirt was missing. I needed it for my run in the park. But the whole family denied taking it. It had simply disappeared. I patted Mitzi as she paced in the hallway. She seemed upset by the mystery, too.

Tell students that the introductions set the stage for the rest of the story, where the writer will tell how the characters solve the mystery. Remind students that they will need to develop their narratives by using dialogue and description. Have students answer these questions as they decide on their topics:

- *Does my narrative topic focus on a manageable mystery?* They should be able to describe the puzzle, complicate it, and solve it in a few pages.

- *Is it a topic I already know about?* Some research may be required, but students should be able to draft some of their mystery using what they already know.

After choosing a mystery, students can plan their narratives. Explain that they need to know their audience and purpose. Understanding why and for whom they are writing will help them shape their narratives and choose their words. Distribute copies of page 41 to students. Tell them to answer the first two questions.

To help them begin gathering ideas, have students record the events and details they have in mind for their narratives on page 41. Have them organize these into *More Important* and *Less Important* categories. This will help them evaluate their plots and determine what parts of their plots may be weak and what research they might need to do to find more details.

© **Grade 4**

CCSS Writing 3.a. Orient the reader by establishing a situation and introducing a narrator and/or characters; organize an event sequence that unfolds naturally.
CCSS Writing 4. Produce clear and coherent writing in which the development and organization are appropriate to task, purpose, and audience.

Writing and Research   23

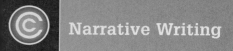

Narrative Writing

Gather Information

Distribute copies of the chart on page 42 to students. Remind them that **research** provides useful information from sources such as print material and Web sites. If students are writing a fictional story, tell them to imagine the setting and the events in their plots and brainstorm details for both. Suggest using dialogue to make the narratives vivid. Point out that students may need to find facts for nonfiction narratives or to support details in fictional narratives. Have students use available sources to locate background information for their narratives. Assist them in finding safe, reliable Web sites. Model how to find facts that add authenticity to their narratives. For example, you might find details about cat behavior on an Internet veterinary medicine site (name of site, Web address). Add any information you find (cats find changes to the environment stressful; cats may act out or have behavioral problems when they have stress.) to the chart.

Allow time for students to research background for their narratives.

Ⓒ **Grade 4**

CCSS Writing 3.b. Use dialogue and description to develop experiences and events or show the responses of characters to situations.

Organize Information

After students have gathered background information and plot ideas, have them organize their narratives by making an **outline.**

Distribute the outline on page 43 to students. Use the following information or information from a selection you've read in class to model how to begin an outline for students.

I. Introduction Maria accuses Jane of taking her favorite sweatshirt; cat Mitzi acting strangely

II. Body

    A. Eliminating suspects at home

        1. Jane "the filcher" didn't take it—not in her room.

        2. Mom didn't put it in the laundry.

        3. It's not in Maria's backpack or the piles in her room.

Point out to students that they may need to add or subtract letters or numbers in the outline to fit their particular information. Remind them to begin by introducing the setting, characters, and problem and to end with the solution of the problem.

Have students write **first drafts** of their narratives, using their outlines to guide them. Encourage them to write quickly without worrying about errors. They will correct mistakes when they revise and edit the writing.

CCSS **Writing 3.e.** Provide a conclusion that follows from the narrated experiences or events. CCSS **Writing 8.** Recall relevant information from experiences or gather relevant information from print and digital sources; take notes and categorize information, and provide a list of sources.

Revise, Edit, and Evaluate Writing

After a first draft is finished, students should polish their narratives using the revision and editing processes. Explain that when they **revise** their writing, students will look at their word choices, sentences, and organization of ideas to make them more effective or to create a mood. They may add, delete, reorder, or change words or sentences. Model, for example, how to replace general words with more precise ones.

Draft: Mitzi had been meowing earlier.

Revision: Mitzi had yowled and paced the hallway for an hour that morning.

Also model reordering sentences to improve the flow of ideas and events.

To **edit** their writing, students will correct errors in spelling, punctuation, capitalization, and grammar. Suggest that students use one or more of the following editing strategies:

- Look for one type of mistake at a time. Make a separate pass through your writing each time. For example, look first for grammar errors, next for capitalization errors, and so on.
- Keep a dictionary handy to check spellings.
- Read the paragraphs aloud or to a partner.
- Place a ruler or card under each line to help focus on the words in that line.

Distribute copies of page 45 to students. Tell them to use the checklists at the top of the page as a guide to what to look for when they revise and edit their first drafts. Allow time for them to revise and edit their writing.

Ask students to write **final drafts** incorporating their revisions and corrections. Then have them answer the questions at the bottom of page 45 to help them evaluate strengths and weaknesses in their writing.

Grade 4

CCSS Writing 5. With guidance and support from peers and adults, develop and strengthen writing as needed by planning, revising, and editing.
CCSS Language 1. Demonstrate command of the conventions of standard English grammar and usage when writing or speaking. CCSS Language 2. Demonstrate command of the conventions of standard English capitalization, punctuation, and spelling when writing.

Publish and Extend Writing

Explain to students that when they will **publish** their writing, they share it with others. Tell students they may choose one of the following ideas for publishing or think of their own ideas.

Ways to Publish

- Read your mystery narrative aloud to a family member, friend, or reading group, using expression to build suspense.

- Illustrate your narrative with original drawings, including an illustrated cover with the title and your name, and add the finished story to the class library.

- Submit your narrative to a mystery-writing contest you have learned about online or through local connections. Share copies with friends and family or share a link if the publication is electronic.

- Work with classmates to create a "Mystery Theater" podcast by recording your narrative and uploading it to a preapproved site, such as the school Web site. Notify friends and family of the link.

Tell students that when they **extend** their writing, they go beyond what they were asked to do in the writing assignment. Offer these ideas for extending, and encourage students to think of and implement their own ideas.

Ways to Extend

- Discuss favorite mysteries with a reading group or group of friends. Point out some techniques of mystery writers and discuss how they help increase suspense or make the problem more complicated.

- Guide younger students in writing their own mystery narratives. Use graphic organizers and other techniques you have learned to help students plan and write.

- Read the narratives of several classmates and select one to review. Evaluate the author's handling of character, setting, and plot. Point out strengths and weaknesses.

- Rewrite the narrative as a play, changing descriptions to stage directions and narration to dialogue. Cast, direct, and perform the play for the class.

© Grade 4

CCSS Writing 6. Use technology, including the Internet, to produce and publish writing as well as to interact and collaborate with others; demonstrate sufficient command of keyboarding skills to type a minimum of three pages in a single sitting. **CCSS Speaking/Listening 1.c.** Pose and respond to specific questions with elaboration and detail by making comments that contribute to the topic, text, or issue under discussion.

UNIT 5: ADVENTURES BY LAND, AIR, AND WATER

Introduce the Writing Assignment

Tell students that they will practice informative/explanatory writing. **Informative/ explanatory writing,** also known as expository writing, gives factual information about a person, place, or thing, or explains how or why things happen. Model ideas suitable for informative/explanatory writing:

Mount Everest is the ultimate challenge for mountain climbers.

Preparing for a deep-sea dive requires several important steps.

Explain that writers often tell about causes and effects to explain a process clearly. They also provide supporting details to clarify a main idea. Informative/explanatory writing requires the use of facts and details to inform and explain.

Brainstorm Topics

As a class, have students brainstorm **topics** they could use for their informative/ explanatory writing. Distribute copies of the web on page 40. Remind students that the theme of Unit 5 is Adventures by Land, Air, and Water, and write *Adventures by Land, Air, and Water* in the center oval. Ask students to think of adventures people can have on land, in the air, and in water. Write their suggestions in the outer ovals of the web. Ask them what makes each experience an adventure. Add these ideas to the adventures in the outer ovals. If necessary, prompt students with questions such as *What challenges might you face if you _____? How would it expand your horizons?*

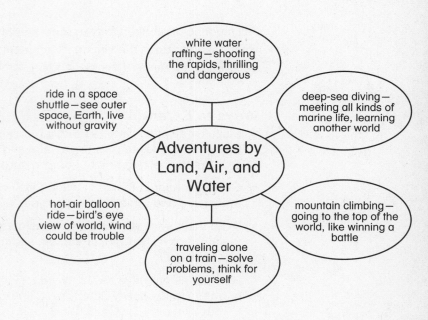

CCSS Writing 2. Write informative/explanatory texts to examine a topic and convey ideas and information clearly. CCSS Speaking Listening 1. Engage effectively in a range of collaborative discussions (one-on-one, in groups, and teacher-led) with diverse partners *on grade 4 topics and texts*, building on others' ideas and expressing their own clearly.

Narrow the Topic

Review the web that the class constructed. Model creating a main idea sentence for one of the topics. For example, "Mount Everest, known as 'The Goddess of the Sky,' is the ultimate challenge for mountain climbers."

Explain that students now need to choose a topic for their writing. They also need to limit, or focus, their topic. Before students choose their topics, have them ask these questions:

- *Is it limited appropriately?* An appropriate topic can be covered adequately in four or five paragraphs.

- *Do I already know some facts about the topic?* They should be able to think of some facts and ideas before they do research.

Once students have chosen a topic, they can begin planning their writing. First, have them think about their audience and purpose for writing. Distribute copies of page 41 to students. Have them answer the first two questions. To encourage them to keep their audience and purpose for writing in mind as they write, have them ask themselves questions such as *Does this information help me achieve my purpose? Will my readers find it interesting? Will they understand these words?*

To help them begin gathering ideas, ask students to jot down several facts and details they can use in their informative/explanatory writing. Then have them organize their ideas into *More Important* and *Less Important* categories. This will help them evaluate their ideas and decide what additional information they need to find through research.

© **Grade 4**

CCSS Writing 4. Produce clear and coherent writing in which the development and organization are appropriate to task, purpose, and audience.

Gather Information

Distribute copies of the chart on page 42 to students. Remind them that **research** provides useful information from sources such as print material and Web sites. Have students use books and the Internet to locate support for the important ideas they want to cover. Assist them in finding safe, reliable Web sites. Model how to record the source information and the details that support the idea that Mount Everest presents climbers with the ultimate challenge (e.g., large support group are necessary, physical conditions, unpredictable weather and events show danger, need to be their best physically and mentally). Model finding facts that show specific ways Mount Everest is challenging. For example, you might find descriptions of the last stages of the climb and physical effects of the climb in an Internet article. Add information about these sources (name of Web site, name of article, name of author, Web address) to the chart. Then record the details that support the main idea (traverse glacial valley, sheer wall of ice; north summit—Hillary Step most challenging of all; summit temperatures average −36 degrees C; hurricane-force winds; frequent avalanches; lack of oxygen; life-threatening symptoms above 26,000 feet) into the chart. Explain what you are doing and why.

Allow time for students to research reasons, details, and facts to use in their informative/explanatory writing.

© Grade 4

CCSS Writing 9. Draw evidence from literary or informational texts to support analysis, reflection, and research. CCSS Writing 2.b. Develop the topic with facts, definitions, concrete details, quotations, or other information and examples related to the topic.

Organize Information

When students have gathered enough facts and details to support their main ideas, have them organize their information by making an **outline.**

Distribute the outline on page 43 to students. Use the following information or information from a selection you've read in class to model how to begin an outline for students.

Topic Adventures by Land, Air, and Water

I. Introduction Mount Everest, known as "The Goddess of the Sky," is the ultimate challenge for mountain climbers.

II. Body

    A. Changes on the mountain threaten lives.

        1. Sudden fierce storms may trap or blind climbers.

        2. Glaciers may shift suddenly, creating deep crevasses.

        3. Avalanches occur often and have killed many.

Point out to students that they may need to add or subtract letters or numbers in the outline to fit their information. Ask them to write a paragraph for the introduction, the conclusion, and each important idea about the topic in their **first drafts.**

© Grade 4

CCSS Writing 2.a. Introduce a topic clearly and group related information in paragraphs and sections; include formatting (e.g., headings), illustrations, and multimedia when useful to aiding comprehension. CCSS Writing 8. Recall relevant information from experiences or gather relevant information from print and digital sources; take notes and categorize information, and provide a list of sources.

Revise, Edit, and Evaluate Writing

Remind students that once they have completed their first drafts, it is time to make their writing more polished. Writers get their ideas on paper in first drafts, but they know that they still need to revise and edit their writing.

Explain that when they **revise** their writing, students will consider ways to improve their word choices, sentences, and organization of ideas. They decide which words or sentences to change, move, or delete. They might add information where they think they didn't explore their ideas adequately. They might replace vague words and phrases with more specific ones. They would move a sentence that is out of order or combine two sentences using a conjunction (*but, so, because, when*) to show that the ideas in the sentences are related.

To **edit** their writing, students will find and correct errors in spelling, punctuation, capitalization, and grammar. Suggest that students use some of the following editing tips:

- Look for one type of mistake at a time. Make a separate pass through the text each time. For example, look first for spelling errors, next for capitalization errors, and finally for grammar errors.
- Use a dictionary to check spellings and forms of words, such as verb tenses.
- Read the paragraphs aloud to themselves or to a partner.
- Place a ruler or card under each line to help focus on the words in that line.

Distribute copies of page 46 to students. Tell them to use the checklists at the top of the page to help them know what to look for as they revise and edit their first drafts. Allow time for them to revise and edit their writing.

Ask students to write **final drafts** incorporating their revisions and corrections. Remind students that this copy of their writing should be legible and neat so that their audience can read it easily. Then have them answer the questions at the bottom of page 46 to help them evaluate strengths and weaknesses in their writing.

© Grade 4

CCSS Writing 5. With guidance and support from peers and adults, develop and strengthen writing as needed by planning, revising, and editing. CCSS Language 1. Demonstrate command of the conventions of standard English grammar and usage when writing or speaking. CCSS Language 2. Demonstrate command of the conventions of standard English capitalization, punctuation, and spelling when writing.

Publish and Extend Writing

Explain to students that now they will **publish** their writing so that they can share it with others. Remind them that there are many different ways to publish written work. Tell students they may choose one of the following ideas for publishing, or they may think of their own ideas.

Ways to Publish

- Read your writing to a friend, classmate, or family member. Ask the listener to tell the main ideas and describe how the writing made him or her feel about the adventure.

- Post your writing on a bulletin board titled "Adventures by Land, Sea, and Air." Contribute to the display by adding illustrations related to the topic to go with your writing.

- Work with classmates to create a class book about adventures. Help organize the writings and prepare a table of contents and cover. Place the book in the school library.

- Submit your writing to the school newspaper. Give copies of the issue to relatives and friends.

- Participate in a group presentation about great adventures by reading your writing aloud. Answer questions from your classmates about the adventure you chose.

Tell students that when they **extend** their writing, they go beyond what they were asked to do in the writing assignment. Offer these ideas for extending, and encourage students to think of and implement their own ideas.

Ways to Extend

- Make a drawing or painting that expresses the physical and mental challenges that make an adventure thrilling. Focus on one theme: land, air, or water adventures.

- Complete the statement "My most incredible adventure so far has been _____" and explain what happened as you talk with a partner. Include details that show why the adventure was exciting or scary or both.

- Make a lesson to teach younger children the process you used for informative/explanatory writing. You can create a graphic organizer to show important points and use examples from your process, such as notes, an outline, and checklists.

- Write a brief skit or news broadcast that communicates the thrill of the adventure from your writing. Work with classmates to prepare and present the skit or broadcast orally.

© Grade 4

CCSS Writing 6. With some guidance and support from adults, use technology, including the Internet, to produce and publish writing as well as to interact and collaborate with others; demonstrate sufficient command of keyboarding skills to type a minimum of one page in a single sitting. CCSS Speaking Listening 1.c. Pose and respond to specific questions to clarify or follow up on information, and make comments that contribute to the discussion and link to the remarks of others.

UNIT 6: REACHING FOR GOALS

Introduce the Writing Assignment

Tell students that they will be writing an opinion. Remind them that an **opinion** is a person's view, belief, or judgment about a subject. Model different opinions about the same topic: *Chance is the biggest reason why inventors succeed because most inventions are created by accident. Inventors succeed because they don't get discouraged by failure.* Opinions cannot be proven true, as facts can. However, opinions can be strengthened or supported by logical reasons and details. Suggest sample reasons and details with students.

Opinion: Inventors succeed as a result of chance.	**Opinion:** Inventors succeed because they don't get discouraged.
Support: Most inventions are created by accident. Penicillin was discovered by accident.	**Support:** Determination is a powerful weapon. Motivation helps you stick with it.

Point out that offering reasons and details for opinions helps writers explain their ideas and persuade others that their opinions are right.

Brainstorm Topics

Remind students that the first step in writing is to select a **topic** to write about. Ask students to brainstorm topic ideas for opinion writing. Distribute copies of page 40 to students. Focus on the theme of Unit 6 by writing *Reaching for Goals* in the center oval. Ask students to name resources or qualities needed to achieve goals. Write their suggestions in the outer ovals of the web. Then elicit examples of reaching for goals that illustrate each suggestion. Prompt with questions such as *Whose achievement made you think of this resource/quality? What action(s)/effort(s) led the person to success?* Encourage students to state their ideas as opinions. Write the opinions in the relevant ovals.

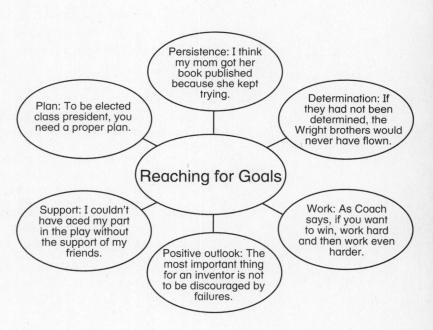

© **Grade 4**

CCSS Writing 1. Write opinion pieces on topics or texts, supporting a point of view with reasons and information. **CCSS Speaking Listening 1.** Engage effectively in a range of collaborative discussions (one-on-one, in groups, and teacher-led) with diverse partners *on grade 4 topics and texts*, building on others' ideas and expressing their own clearly.

Narrow the Topic

Display the web that the class constructed, reviewing the opinions. Tell what makes each statement an opinion. Point out words that signal opinions such as *think, never, most important,* and *need*. Explain that such words point to personal beliefs or judgments.

Explain that students now need to choose a topic to write about. As they view the list of possible topics, students need to ask themselves:

- *Is the topic limited enough for opinion writing? Can it be covered adequately in four or five paragraphs?* If not, it may be too general.

- *Do I already know something about the topic?* Even before they begin their research, they should be able to think of some supporting reasons and details.

Once students choose their topics, have them start planning their writing by identifying their audience and purpose for writing. Distribute copies of page 41 to students and have them answer the first two questions. Explain that they should keep in mind whom they are writing for and what they want to accomplish as they plan and write their first drafts.

Next, students need to begin organizing their reasons and details. After they write the reasons and details they have in mind, have them sort their support into *More Important* and *Less Important* categories. This process will help them evaluate the strength of their reasons and details and decide how much research they need to do to find more.

© Grade 4

CCSS Writing 1.a. Introduce a topic or text clearly, state an opinion, and create an organizational structure in which related ideas are grouped to support the writer's purpose. **CCSS Writing 1.b.** Provide reasons that are supported by facts and details. **CCSS Writing 4.** Produce clear and coherent writing in which the development and organization are appropriate to task, purpose, and audience.

Gather Information

Distribute copies of the chart on page 42 to students. Remind them that **research** provides useful information from sources such as print material and Web sites. To help students locate support for their opinions, guide them to current print material and reliable Web sites. Model by finding facts that support the opinion "Inventors succeed because they aren't discouraged by failure," such as examples of failures in a biography of an inventor or an Internet summary. Add information about these sources (name of book, author's name, page number(s); Web site name, title and author of text, Web address) to the chart. Then record the information that supports the opinion (Edison tested 10,000 substances to find the filament material for his light bulb. He said, "I have not failed. I've just found 10,000 ways that will not work.") into the chart. Explain what you are doing and why.

Allow time for students to research reasons, details, and facts to use in their opinion writing.

CCSS Writing 9. Draw evidence from literary or informational texts to support analysis, reflection, and research.

Organize Information

When students judge that they have gathered enough reasons, details, and facts to support their opinions, have them organize their information by making an **outline.**

Distribute the outline on page 44 to students. Use the following information or information from a selection you've read in class to model how to begin an outline for students.

Topic Reaching for Goals

Opinion Inventors succeed because they don't get discouraged by failure.

    A. Reason 1 They know failures help them learn and move forward.

        1. Supporting detail Thomas Edison tried 10,000 substances before finding that a carbon filament glowed many hours in the electric light bulb.

        2. Supporting detail Steve Wozniak learned to try something, find out why it didn't work, and try something else using the knowledge gained.

Tell students that they may need to add or subtract letters or numbers from the outline to fit their information. Next, have students use their outlines to write the **first drafts** of their opinions. Remind them that they should develop a paragraph for the introduction, a paragraph for the conclusion, and a paragraph for each reason that supports their opinion.

CCSS Writing 8. Recall relevant information from experiences or gather relevant information from print and digital sources; take notes and categorize information, and provide a list of sources.

Revise, Edit, and Evaluate Writing

Remind students that in their first drafts, they captured their ideas on paper without worrying about mistakes or missing parts. Now that they have finished writing their first drafts, they need to revise and edit their writing before making final copies.

Explain that when they **revise** their writing, students evaluate their word choices, sentences, and organization of ideas. They may decide to add, delete, reorder, or change words or sentences. For example, they would delete any text that is irrelevant to the topic. They might add phrases that show the order or relationship of ideas (*the next stage, in the same way, in conclusion*). They would replace vague words (such as *bad, did*) with more precise ones (such as *discouraged, tinkered*).

When they **edit** their writing, students find and fix errors in spelling, punctuation, capitalization, and grammar. Suggest that students use some of the following editing strategies and model them as needed:

- Make several passes through the draft, focusing on looking for one kind of error each time.
- Use a dictionary to check spellings.
- Read the writing aloud to a partner.
- Place a ruler or card under each line to help focus on the words in that line.

Distribute copies of page 47 to students. Tell them to use the checklists at the top of the page to help guide their revision and editing process. Allow time for them to revise and edit their writing.

Ask students to write **final drafts** incorporating their revisions and corrections. Then have them answer the questions at the bottom of page 47 to help them identify what they like about their writing and what they want to improve.

Ⓒ Grade 4

CCSS Writing 5. With guidance and support from peers and adults, develop and strengthen writing as needed by planning, revising, and editing. CCSS Language 1. Demonstrate command of the conventions of standard English grammar and usage when writing or speaking. CCSS Language 2. Demonstrate command of the conventions of standard English capitalization, punctuation, and spelling when writing.

Publish and Extend Writing

Explain to students that the final step is to **publish** their writing so that they can share it with others. Remind them that there are many different ways to publish written work. Offer the following possibilities to students, and explain that they may use one of their own ideas instead.

Ways to Publish

- Read your opinion writing aloud to classmates or family members. Ask your listeners to tell whether they agree with the opinion and explain why they did or did not find it convincing.

- Add illustrations to support or clarify important ideas in your writing. Display the finished work on a poster or bulletin board.

- Present your writing as an oral report or dramatic reading, using objects or graphics to support your opinion and reasons.

- Submit your opinion writing to the school newspaper. Share copies of the newspaper with relatives and friends.

- Work with classmates to create a class book of opinion writing about achieving goals. Help design and create a cover, organize the content, and make a table of contents. Display the book in the school library.

Tell students that when they **extend** their writing, they go beyond what they were asked to do in the writing assignment. Offer the following ideas for extending, and encourage students to think of and implement their own ideas.

Ways to Extend

- Tell a partner how you worked to achieve a goal and why you believe you succeeded. Take turns stating an opinion and the reasons you have for it.

- Use your opinion writing as the starting point for a journal about personal goals. Continue making entries about what you are doing to achieve a particular goal.

- Survey classmates about the goal you think is most important for students. Identify the top three goals of students in your class, express them as opinions, and show the statistical results in a graphic.

- Work with other students to create a one-act play about achieving a goal. Feature several qualities necessary to achieve the goal. Prepare and present the play to classmates.

© Grade 4

CCSS Writing 6. With some guidance and support from adults, use technology, including the Internet, to produce and publish writing as well as to interact and collaborate with others; demonstrate sufficient command of keyboarding skills to type a minimum of one page in a single sitting. **CCSS Speaking Listening 1.c.** Pose and respond to specific questions to clarify or follow up on information, and make comments that contribute to the discussion and link to the remarks of others.

Use the web to help you think of possible topics and to choose the topic you will write about.

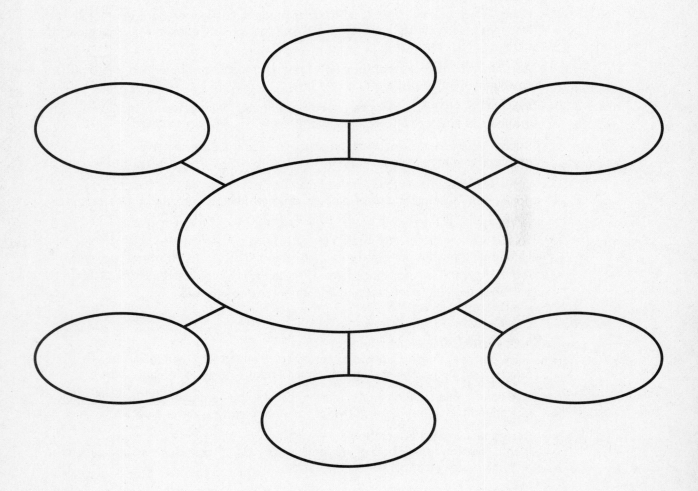

Copyright © Pearson Education, Inc., or its affiliates. All Rights Reserved. 4

Name _____

Thinking about your audience and your purpose for writing will help you as you plan your writing. Answer these questions.

1. For whom are you writing? _____

_____

This is your **audience**.

2. What do you want your audience to know? _____

_____

This is your **purpose** for writing.

Think about the ideas and details you already know that you want to use in your writing and how you will organize them.

Write the ideas and details here.

Organize the ideas and details here.

More Important	Less Important

Copyright © Pearson Education, Inc., or its affiliates. All Rights Reserved. 4

Name _____

Write the information and the sources where you found the information in the chart.

Source	Information

Copyright © Pearson Education, Inc., or its affiliates. All Rights Reserved. 4

Name _____

Fill in the outline with the ideas and details for your writing. You may need to add or delete numbers or letters. Write on another sheet of paper if you need more space.

I. Introduction

_____

_____

II. Body

A. _____

1. _____

2. _____

B. _____

1. _____

2. _____

_____

C. _____

1. _____

2. _____

III.   Conclusion

_____

_____

Copyright © Pearson Education, Inc., or its affiliates. All Rights Reserved. 4

Name _____

Fill in the outline with the information you have gathered. You may need to add or delete numbers or letters. Write on another sheet of paper if you need more space.

I. Introduction

Topic _____

Opinion _____

II. Body

A. Reason 1 _____

   1. Supporting Detail _____

   2. Supporting Detail _____

B. Reason 2 _____

   1. Supporting Detail _____

   2. Supporting Detail _____

C. Reason 3 _____

   1. Supporting Detail _____

   2. Supporting Detail _____

III. Conclusion

Restate Topic and Opinion _____

Summarize Reasons _____

Copyright © Pearson Education, Inc., or its affiliates. All Rights Reserved. 4

Name _____

Use the checklists to revise and edit your first draft.
Check *Yes* or *No* for each statement.

Revise	Yes	No
1. I introduced my characters and setting at the beginning.		
2. I developed the problem through the events in my plot.		
3. I resolved the problem by the end of my narrative.		

Edit	Yes	No
4. I made sure all my words were spelled correctly.		
5. I capitalized proper nouns and used end punctuation.		
6. I used verbs that agreed with the subjects of my sentences.		

Use the questions to evaluate your final draft. Write your answers

in complete sentences.

7. What is the best part of your writing? Why do you think that?

8. What could you change to make your writing more entertaining for readers? How would that help?

Copyright © Pearson Education, Inc., or its affiliates. All Rights Reserved. 4

Use the checklists to revise and edit your first draft.
Check *Yes* or *No* for each statement.

Revise	Yes	No
1. I stated my topic in my introduction.		
2. I wrote about one main idea in each paragraph in the body.		
3. I summarized my ideas in my conclusion.		

Edit	Yes	No
4. I used a dictionary to check any new words I used.		
5. I began every sentence with a capital letter.		
6. I checked to be sure I included small words such as *to* and *the*.		

Use the questions to evaluate your final draft. Write your answers
in complete sentences.

7. What is the best part of your writing? Why do you think that?
8. What could you change to make your writing easier for readers to understand? How would that help?

Copyright © Pearson Education, Inc., or its affiliates. All Rights Reserved. 4

Name _____

Use the checklists to revise and edit your first draft.
Check *Yes* or *No* for each statement.

Revise	Yes	No
1. I stated my opinion in my introduction.		
2. I wrote one paragraph for each reason supporting my opinion.		
3. I included at least two details to support each reason.		

Edit	Yes	No
4. I spelled all the words correctly.		
5. I used commas correctly in series and after clauses.		
6. I used the correct forms of pronouns.		

Use the questions to evaluate your final draft.
Write your answers in complete sentences.

7. What is the best part of your opinion writing? Why do you think that?

8. What could you change to make your opinion writing more convincing to readers? How would that help?

Copyright © Pearson Education, Inc., or its affiliates. All Rights Reserved. 4